About the Author

Kirsten Smith created the *Find Fix Forward* program as a means of helping people find their true happiness within relationships. She pulled from her psychology background as well as her experience in business coaching and consulting to craft a program designed to help people understand and express themselves in a more profound way, thus fostering future fulfilment and satisfaction. She loves absurdity, musical theater, and dogs with middle names. She hates the sound of Styrofoam, wet sweaters, and stairs that are too long or too short. Visit her at www.findfixforward.com to learn about this program and others.

The Unbreakable Couple

15 exercises to achieve security, stability and satisfaction in your relationship

Kirsten Smith

The Unbreakable Couple
15 exercises to achieve security, stability
and satisfaction in your relationship

Olympia Publishers
London

www.olympiapublishers.com
OLYMPIA PAPERBACK EDITION

A CIP catalogue record for this title is
available from the British Library.

ISBN: 978-1-80074-122-5

First Published in 2021

**Olympia Publishers
Tallis House
2 Tallis Street
London
EC4Y 0AB**

Printed in Great Britain

Dedication

To Andrew, for constantly inspiring, motivating, challenging, teaching, supporting, encouraging, and loving me. You always stand in front of, beside, or behind me, whenever I need it most, and you have taught me the true meaning of what a partner should be. I love you endlessly.

Welcome!

If you are reading this, you are clearly invested in making your relationship the best it can be! Whether you are a new couple looking to establish a solid foundation and boundaries for your future success, or you are a couple experiencing frustrations far into the relationship, these exercises will help you achieve clarity, understanding, and, ultimately, satisfaction in your relationship.

Taking the first step in this journey is undeniably positive, but it may also feel intimidating. The exercises in this book are designed specifically to take the stress out of having difficult discussions with your partner, with guided instructions for what to share, how to express yourself, and how to reflect on your discussions afterward to give you the highest level of clarity. When both partners have the time and space to fully think through what they want to share and they share it in a space that is welcoming and open, real communication happens. This step is courageous, so congratulations on your commitment to working towards becoming unbreakable. Let's get started!

Why Relationships Struggle

Relationships can take a negative turn for many reasons. Often, we try to address the symptoms that are easy to pick out — a partner doesn't spend enough time at home, a partner no longer shows affection, etc. — and come up with solutions for them. Addressing these symptoms is like putting a bandage on a deep wound without addressing the reason for the bleeding. We need to dig deep to determine the issues that are actually causing the problems between you and your partner to come up with solutions for achieving more successful outcomes. To do this, we need to first evaluate what the real root of the problem is. Below are several common reasons that relationships begin to break down. For new couples, these are the issues you are here to avoid! For established couples, some of these may sound familiar and we will tackle them all through the exercises.

1) We have different desired relationship styles.

There are many types of relationship styles. Some couples may work together to tackle everything as a team, while others prefer to delegate specific tasks and share the duties. Some prefer a "leader and follower" style, where still others prefer to just go with the flow and address problems as they come. Every relationship is different, and that's okay! Problems occur when one partner wants one relationship style and the other partner prefers a different one. This leads to tension about responsibilities, expectations, and teamwork. It can also result in one partner trying to change the other to fit a mould. It also most often results in two unsatisfied and frustrated partners.

2) We aren't able to express what we want or need.

This could come from not fully knowing what it is you want, or it could have developed over time due to built-up defences and resentment. Partners who do not feel comfortable expressing what they want often begin to resent their partners for not providing them with what they want, although the simple lack of communication may be the thing stopping it from happening! If this is happening, we may withdraw from the conversations or relationship as a whole, as a means of protecting ourselves and looking out for our own best interests instead of the interests of the relationship.

3) One partner starts putting themselves first (or both of them do).

Whether this is a tendency of the individual or a learned trait inside of the relationship caused by negative experiences or events, this is a relationship destroyer. Partners experiencing this tend not to show empathy towards their partners during difficult situations, instead only thinking about how it affects themselves. This can also result from one partner feeling that their interests are not a consideration of the other partner and can lead to them developing this trait to protect themselves. However it develops, it leads to partners feeling alone, misunderstood, and always on the defensive. When one partner is only focused on the best outcome for themselves and the other is doing the same, no one is thinking about the best outcome for the relationship.

4) Resentment is built up over time and changes us.

Over time, a lot of things will happen in a relationship that may cause hurt feelings. From simple offhand comments, to big, monumental actions and arguments, these things tend to build up. Even if we think we let them go, a part of them may remain with us, causing us to harden towards our partner. It makes us less forgiving, more apt to shift blame, and more likely to look for problems where they may not exist.

5) *We assume bad intent from our partners.*

This is often seen as trying to "read between the lines." That is, what is my partner actually trying to say when they say/do this? When we go down this path, we often end up with an assumption of their intent that is not positive. "Have you done this?" becomes "why haven't you done this yet?" Assuming bad intent is one of the biggest causes of unnecessary arguments. It causes hurt feelings, misunderstanding, resentment, and worry — often for no reason. We may assume negative intent if we are feeling insecure or if the relationship has a history of friction, but allowing this assumed intent to guide your responses and reactions will most certainly result in dissatisfaction.

One or more of these statements may ring true to you immediately, but it is likely that some of the other ones are having an effect, even if you aren't conscious of it at this moment. Even the happiest couples face into these issues (and others!) on a regular basis — they just may be more successful at addressing them instead of allowing them to build up. Through this book, you will get the tools you need to diagnose your relationship to determine which of these issues (or others) are getting in your way, and how to avoid them if you have yet to experience them.

What You Will Get

The "Find" Process
Ultimately, this book will provide you clarity that will help you to more deeply understand yourself and your relationship. This can help you to avoid issues before they arise, or it can help you to make necessary adjustments to help your relationship heal and prosper. Through a host of exercises, you will get a clearer picture about yourself, your partner, and your relationship. You will be able to examine what is working, what changes need to be made, and how to ask for or discuss these changes. You will be asked to dig deep into the reasons, motivations, and drivers that affect your relationship from all sides, then come up with solutions for how to move forward successfully.

The "Fix" Process
After you have worked to uncover the things potentially getting in the way of your relationship, you can begin discussing them clearly and effectively (without fighting!). Each section designated as a "teamwork exercise" will contain an exercise to be completed individually along with targeted instructions for how to share your reflections with your partner. These sharing sessions will allow for open communication and sharing without the potential for arguments or defences being put up. You will have time to

gather all of your thoughts before the discussion so that you feel fully prepared and never put "on the spot." Allowing yourself to be vulnerable and open with your partner during these exercises will help you to move towards greater understanding and fulfilment.

The "Forward" Process

By achieving clarity on what you want as individuals and as a couple, you will be able to evaluate what needs to be done to create greater satisfaction for both partners. As a result of the exercises and sharing sessions, you will come up with a series of action plans, both for yourselves individually and together as a team. You will also establish a game plan for not only addressing issues you currently face, but also issues that arise in the future. This action plan will allow you to move forward together, ever closer to your version of the ideal relationship.

Each exercise will be labelled as "individual exercise" or "team exercise." Individual exercises are meant to be completed alone and not shared between partners, as they are intended solely for personal reflection. Some exercises will offer the option of being completed on our website in order for your final program to be customized to your relationship, and I highly recommend that you take advantage of this opportunity. It will allow you to be completely honest and vulnerable without the concern of having to express your direct feedback to your partner before you are ready. Exercises labelled "team exercise" will be completed individually by each partner and then followed by a sharing session and reflection exercise afterwards. Clear instructions will be given for how the sharing session should take place for each exercise, but the common thread is that sharing sessions are meant for listening, not debating. It is often said that people listen in order to respond, but this will not be the case here, and for good reason. There is a lot of power in just focusing on hearing what your partner is sharing with you instead of thinking about how you are going to respond or defend your position. Once you have both shared, you will go to a separate space and take time to reflect on what you heard and what your next steps are. Taking this separate time allows emotions to cool and each partner to think clearly and deeply about the situation, hopefully equally from both perspectives.

Each exercise will show up in its entirety in each chapter. You can choose to complete the exercises in your own copies of the book so that you can keep your responses separate and compiled, or you can print additional copies of the exercises from our website and have one partner complete their exercises that way. By visiting our page at www.findfixforward.com, you will be able to learn more about our programs and purchase additional coaching for the duration of your program if you so choose. When you're ready, grab a pen, let your guard down, and dive in!

The State of The Relationship

The first step to figuring out how to get to where you want to go is to determine where you are. In this individual exercise, you will both evaluate your opinion of the current state of your relationship and reflect on what is working and what could be improved upon. We will establish an "ideal state" to work towards and make sure that your future conversations and revelations move you closer to this goal. This is not meant to be shared with your partner, but rather for you both to be completely open and honest about what is happening. This will help to establish a starting point for your journey, and will allow you to reflect back later once you have put in all of the hard work! We will not yet get into the causes, just the observations. On the lines below or on your printed copy, answer the following questions. For each question, there are guides to help you fully understand what is being asked and answer it fully, although it is not important to answer each of the guiding questions individually.

For additional copies of this exercise, visit www.findfixforward.com/resources and click on Exercise 1.

1) What does your ideal relationship look like?

Describe your idea of the perfect relationship. How much time would you spend together? How much time should you spend apart? How should you split up household duties? Do you want to lead, follow, or be equal? How do you treat and support each other?

_____

_____

_____

_____

_____

_____

_____

2) Think of a couple you admire. It could be a real couple you know or a fictitious couple. What do you admire about their relationship? What qualities do they have that you would like to have in your own relationship?

_____

_____

_____

_____

_____

3) What aspects of your current relationship are your version of ideal?

Is the amount of time you spend together ideal? What about the way in which you support each other or offer advice? What about the way you share tasks? What makes your relationship something you want to fight for?

_____

_____

_____

_____

_____

_____

4) What aspects of your relationship would you like to improve?

Where do you feel there are misalignments in the relationship? Does one partner seem to have a goal that the other doesn't share? Do you communicate, fight, or share tasks unsuccessfully?

_____

_____

_____

_____

_____

_____

_____

5) What do you think is getting in the way of your relationship being fully ideal?

Is there an issue with communication, boundaries, expectations, or goals? Describe what is getting in the way. What about it makes it a problem? Can this be changed?

_____

_____

_____

_____

_____

_____

_____

6) What would need to happen in order for this barrier to be removed?

Would better communication help, or would you need to come up with a compromise to solve a problem you don't agree upon?

_____

_____

_____

_____

_____

_____

7) How would you describe the role that you play in your relationship?

What are you responsible for? Do you handle the financials, household chores, parenting duties, or provide moral support? Are you the planner? What value do you bring to the relationship?

_____

_____

_____

_____

_____

_____

8) How would you describe the role that your partner plays in your relationship?

What is your partner responsible for? Do they handle the financials, household chores, parenting duties, or provide moral support? Are they the planner? What value do they bring to the relationship?

_____

_____

_____

_____

_____

_____

9) How often do you argue with your partner?

Do you argue daily over little things, or is it saved up for larger fights less frequently? How often do those happen?

_____

_____

_____

_____

_____

_____

_____

10) What are your big fights about?

These are often the main issues from your relationship that may boil over from time to time.

_____

_____

_____

_____

_____

_____

_____

11) What are your little fights about?

These are the smaller, seemingly insignificant day-to-day fights that may uncover deeper issues at play.

_____

_____

_____

_____

_____

_____

_____

12) When you argue with your partner, how do you behave (actions)?

Do you yell? Do you escalate the situation? Do you back down and give in to get out of the argument? Do you say hurtful things that you regret afterwards?

_____

_____

_____

_____

_____

_____

_____

13) When you argue with your partner, how do they behave (actions)?

Do they yell? Do they escalate the situation? Do they back down and give in to get out of the argument? Do they say hurtful things?

_____

_____

_____

_____

_____

_____

14) What do you hope to gain through this program?

Do you hope to achieve a deeper understanding of yourself and how you behave in the relationship? Or are you more concerned with learning to communicate better? Do you just want to stop the constant arguments?

_____

_____

_____

Positive Traits and Experiences

Part 1:

You fell in love with your partner for a reason. Although those reasons may have become overshadowed by everyday frustrations and resentment, they are still there, or at the least the hope of them is still there. They are what draws you back together, despite arguments or misunderstandings. What are those reasons? What do you love about your partner, and what brought you together? When things feel tense in a relationship, sometimes taking a step back and looking at the relationship from a different perspective can change your outlook, so spending more time talking about the positives can make a big impact. For this exercise, the more the better, so grab a pen and get to writing! Try to write at least ten traits that your partner possesses.

    For additional copies of this exercise, visit www.findfixforward.com/resources and click on Exercise 2.

Positive Traits

1._____
2._____
3._____
4._____

5._____

6._____

7._____

8._____

9._____

10._____

Part 2:

Next, think about the things you have done together; the things you have experienced as a couple. Take the time to remember some of your greatest hits, and jot down your favourite memories. Maybe it was the first day you met, your first date, your wedding, or a special trip together. Come up with your five favourite positive experiences you shared together, and write a quick summary of the points that meant the most to you. Why were they important? What details do you remember? What feelings did you have as you experienced it? What memories linger the most?

Experience	Memories
1.	
2.	
3.	
4.	
5.	

Team Share

We are going to get into sharing feedback to work towards improvement later, but for now just take some time to just relax and appreciate each other. Schedule a time to sit down together to share your responses to parts 1 and 2 of this exercise. Enjoy hearing the stories you shared and re-living them together from your partner's perspective. Feel free to elaborate on the positive traits or experiences you listed, but I encourage you to first read out loud what you wrote verbatim in this exercise. We often talk about our partners to other people in a way that we don't express to them personally, and it can be very powerful to hear the words you both used when relating the positive experiences in your individual exercises. The language you used when completing your exercise individually may mean a lot to your partner.

Reflection

After you and your partner share your positive traits and experiences, take some time to reflect on what you heard.

- How did that experience feel?

_____

_____

_____

_____

_____

_____

- Did any of your partner's responses surprise you?

_____

_____

_____

_____

_____

- What can you take from this exercise?

_____

_____

_____

_____

_____

Forward Focus

Make a plan for sharing your happy memories together more often.

Couple spotlight: Mark and Tania pick one day each month to re-live an event in their life together. They look at pictures, tell stories, and try to do their best to recreate the experience through food, environment, music, etc.

Needs and Wants

Compromise isn't a bad word. However, there is a big difference in compromising over what you eat for dinner or where you go on vacation and what you want out of life. A lot of people end up compromising on the things they really care about and the things they truly want in order to stay with a partner they have committed to. There is always give and take in a relationship, but at some point it's important for each person to "zoom out" from the relationship and analyse whether they are getting what they really need and want out of their life.

Now, we are going to identify what you really want out of life, and what you are willing to compromise on. In the boxes below or on your printed page, come up with a list of things you desire. These should be your personal goals, not necessarily tied to a relationship. Make sure that they are achievable, not related to things you wish would or could have been. There is room for two goals in each box, for a total of eight, but feel free to print more pages if you have more goals!

For additional copies of this exercise, visit www.findfixforward.com/resources and click on Exercise 3.

For each of the items in your list, answer the following questions:

1) What is the need/want?

Describe, in detail, the thing you would like to achieve. It could be an achievement, a milestone, or a state of being. For example: I want to live in New York. Or, I need to have a family of my own.

2) Is it a need or want?

How important is it to you? If you didn't achieve this, would you feel unfulfilled with your life? If so, it may be a need. Otherwise, it may be a want that you have some ability to compromise on. Understanding your elasticity on these items is essential to determine what you need to fight for and what you may accept giving up for your partner.

3) What about it makes it desirable to you?

Reflecting on the importance of your goal is valuable in determining if the goal itself is important or just the result. For example, if my goal was to get married, I may write that the things that make it desirable are commitment and stability. Then, try to dig deeper. What about those things are desirable? I may say that they provide me with a sense of security that I won't be left alone. Once you uncover the real root of your desire, you may realize that the end result (getting married) doesn't necessarily give you the result (not being alone) that you were hoping for, or it may not be the only way to achieve that goal and you may want to consider other ways to accomplish this.

4) What would achieving this mean to you?

If you achieved this goal, what would that tell you? Would you have reached the pinnacle of your career aspirations, for example? What would you get out of it? How would you benefit by achieving this?

5) What is your role in achieving it?

What actions do you personally have to take to work towards achieving this? How attainable is it?

6) Do you have a timeline for this goal?

Is this something you want to achieve before a certain age? Is it a short-term or long-term goal?

7) Does your partner support it? What have they done to make you feel they support it or not?

For example: "I know my partner supports my goal of having children because we have spoken about it on many occasions and they want children as well." Or "I don't know if my partner supports my goal of becoming an opera singer because we have never discussed it, but they always encourage me to pursue my goals and go out of their way to support me."

8) What does supportive partner behaviour look like to you for this item?

For this question, don't think about what your partner is or is not doing currently. Think about the ideal partner behaviour that would show you that they support you in this pursuit. For example: To support me in my goal of becoming a professional gymnast, my partner would understand the long hours of practicing and not complain about me not wanting to go eat burgers all the time or being away from home. They would tell me they are proud of the work I'm putting in and come to my competitions to show their support.

Goal	Need or Want?	What Makes it Desirable	What Would Achieving it Mean?	What is Your Role?	Timeline	Does Your Partner Support it?	What Does Supportive Behaviour Look Like?

Goal	Need or Want?	What Makes it Desirable	What Would Achieving it Mean?	What is Your Role?	Timeline	Does Your Partner Support it?	What Does Supportive Behaviour Look Like?

Goal	Need or Want?	What Makes it Desirable	What Would Achieving it Mean?	What is Your Role?	Timeline	Does Your Partner Support it?	What Does Supportive Behaviour Look Like?

Goal	Need or Want?	What Makes it Desirable	What Would Achieving it Mean?	What is Your Role?	Timeline	Does Your Partner Support it?	What Does Supportive Behaviour Look Like?

Team Share

The intention behind this exercise is to re-focus on what it is you really desire and to think about how you and your partner can work together to accomplish those goals. The next step is for you to get on the same page and make sure that you have the same ideas in mind for how to accomplish those things! For this to happen, you will both need to be really open about what you want and also what you expect from each other. Work with your partner to put aside some time without distractions where you can share your needs and wants. The structure of the conversation should follow this outline:

One partner shares:

1) I feel the need (or want) to:

_____

(Share what the goal is and specify whether it is a need or want)

2) I need/want this because:

_____

(Share why is it important and what achieving it would mean to you)

3) I would like to accomplish this by:

_____

(Share your desired timeline)

4) For this to happen, I need to:

_____

(Share what your role is in achieving your goal)

5) What supportive partner behaviour looks like for this to me is:

_____

(Share what being supportive means to you with respect to this goal)

6) Is this something you want to prioritize today, or is it something you would like to work towards together in the future? (This could be something you want now but acknowledge it may need to wait).

Then the other partner will share an item. Take turns until your lists are complete.

When sharing each item, try to keep it just about you and avoid accusatory language. You don't need to discuss what your partner is or is not doing to support this goal, just the actions you would expect to see from a supportive partner.

This next part is very important: after you both share, the other partner should NOT respond. This should not lead to a discussion or a debate over what has been done or tried. Your job is to share your feelings about your personal needs and wants and to listen to your partners without judgment. After the conversation, there will be a follow up exercise that will allow you to reflect on what you learned and what your next steps will be.

Reflection

After your sharing session, take some time to think through and reflect on what you heard from your partner. Did you learn anything that surprised you? Did they seem particularly passionate about specific goals? Really take the time to analyse what they said and how they expressed it. Then, make an action plan for how you can help to support them in achieving this goal. Make sure that your plan is manageable and reasonable so that you can follow through.

For each of their items, answer the following questions:

Goal 1: _____

1) What did you hear/learn from your partner concerning this need?

_____

_____

_____

2) Did it surprise you?

    Yes   No

3) Is this a priority or a "work towards later" item?

    Priority   Work Towards Later

4) What actionable steps can you take to support your partner in this?

_____

_____

_____

_____

_____

Goal 2: _____

1) What did you hear/learn from your partner concerning this need?

_____

_____

_____

2) Did it surprise you?

    Yes   No

3) Is this a priority or a "work towards later" item?

    Priority   Work Towards Later

4) What actionable steps can you take to support your partner in this?

_____

_____

_____

Goal 3: _____

1) What did you hear/learn from your partner concerning this need?

_____

_____

_____

2) Did it surprise you?

    Yes   No

3) Is this a priority or a "work towards later" item?

    Priority   Work Towards Later

4) What actionable steps can you take to support your partner in this?

_____

_____

_____

Goal 4: _____

1) What did you hear/learn from your partner concerning this need?

_____

_____

_____

2) Did it surprise you?

    Yes   No

3) Is this a priority or a "work towards later" item?

    Priority   Work Towards Later

4) What actionable steps can you take to support your partner in this?

_____

_____

_____

Goal 5: _____

1) What did you hear/learn from your partner concerning this need?

_____

_____

_____

2) Did it surprise you?

Yes   No

3) Is this a priority or a "work towards later" item?

Priority   Work Towards Later

4) What actionable steps can you take to support your partner in this?

_____

_____

_____

Goal 6: _____

1) What did you hear/learn from your partner concerning this need?

_____

_____

_____

2) Did it surprise you?

Yes   No

3) Is this a priority or a "work towards later" item?

Priority   Work Towards Later

4) What actionable steps can you take to support your partner in this?

_____

_____

_____

Goal 7: _____

1) What did you hear/learn from your partner concerning this need?

_____

_____

_____

2) Did it surprise you?

    Yes   No

3) Is this a priority or a "work towards later" item?

    Priority   Work Towards Later

4) What actionable steps can you take to support your partner in this?

_____

_____

_____

Goal 8: _____

1) What did you hear/learn from your partner concerning this need?

_____

_____

_____

2) Did it surprise you?

    Yes   No

3) Is this a priority or a "work towards later" item?

    Priority   Work Towards Later

4) What actionable steps can you take to support your partner in this?

_____

_____

_____

Were there any common threads that you noticed, where addressing one thing would allow you to have impact on more than one of the needs/wants discussed?

_____

_____

_____

_____

_____

Forward Focus

Come up with your "couple sharing style" to discuss needs and wants on an ongoing basis that feels most comfortable to you and allows you to keep these things in the forefront.

Couple spotlight: At the end of each week, Alex and Robbie sit down to share how they felt the week went in terms of support. They express gratitude for the actions their partner took that made them feel supported, and offer suggestions for what could be helpful moving forward.

Partner Traits

Note: You may choose to complete this exercise one of two ways.

1) Read the directions below and then go to www.findfixforward.com/traits to fill out the form. Both partners should complete their form separately, and the information will be used to begin building your final customized program. *This is the recommended way.*

2) Complete the exercise on the lines below (and print extra copies), as with the previous exercises. The information you write should be kept private, as it is meant for personal reflection unless otherwise indicated.

For additional copies of this exercise, visit www.findfixforward.com/resources and click on Exercise 4.

What you want out of a partner may have changed significantly over time, but it is important to know which traits are your driving traits. You may care less now about finding a partner that looks similar to your favourite Hollywood star, but you may be more consistent on traits such as sense of humour, intelligence, motivation, and desire to have a family.

Develop a list of fifteen traits that your ideal partner should have. Below is a list of examples that you can select from, but I encourage you to come up with your own. Select the ones that are the most important to you, even though most of the traits listed below may be desirable in a partner. Some of the example traits may seem similar, but try to make sure you are purposeful in which one you select. For example, "funny" and "witty" may both describe people with a good sense of humour, but "funny" could describe a person who tells jokes while "witty" could describe a person who uses intelligent humour. In the same way, "good sense of humour" could describe a person who enjoys humour but isn't funny themselves. Try to really get to the root of the traits that appeal to you most. Once you have developed your list of desired traits, rank them in order of importance to you. Place the most important trait on line 1, working up in order through line 15. Then, consider how much your partner possesses that trait. Give them a rating of 1-5, with 1 being "never exhibits that trait" and 5 being "always exhibits that trait."

Sample List: They respect you, Smart, Funny, Empathetic, Supportive, Attractive, Shares my political beliefs, Wants a family, Wants to have children, They push you to do/be more, Honest, Trustworthy, Understanding, Dependable, Shares my religious beliefs, Shared values, High Sex Drive, Emotional intelligence, Forgiving, They are passionate about things, Willing to compromise, Driven/ambitious, Faithful, Willing to change/improve, Independent, Not controlling, Makes you feel appreciated, Makes you feel adored, Expressive, They turn you on, Witty, Cares about family, Generous, Lets me focus on my passions, Financially stable, Physically Fit, Responsible, Romantic, Sweet, Kind, Thoughtful, Educated

Positive Traits

	Never Exhibits This Trait		*Sometimes Exhibits This Trait*		*Always Exhibits This Trait*
Most Important Trait: _____	*1*	*2*	*3*	*4*	*5*
Trait 2: _____	*1*	*2*	*3*	*4*	*5*
Trait 3: _____	*1*	*2*	*3*	*4*	*5*
Trait 4: _____	*1*	*2*	*3*	*4*	*5*
Trait 5: _____	*1*	*2*	*3*	*4*	*5*
Trait 6: _____	*1*	*2*	*3*	*4*	*5*
Trait 7: _____	*1*	*2*	*3*	*4*	*5*
Trait 8: _____	*1*	*2*	*3*	*4*	*5*
Trait 9: _____	*1*	*2*	*3*	*4*	*5*

Trait 10: _____	*1*	*2*	*3*	*4*	*5*
Trait 11: _____	*1*	*2*	*3*	*4*	*5*
Trait 12: _____	*1*	*2*	*3*	*4*	*5*
Trait 13: _____	*1*	*2*	*3*	*4*	*5*
Trait 14: _____	*1*	*2*	*3*	*4*	*5*
Trait 15: _____	*1*	*2*	*3*	*4*	*5*

Next, come up with a list of traits that you definitely DON'T want in a partner. These may turn you off, gross you out, cause a loss of motivation or stimulation, or embarrass you. Similar to the last exercise, examples are provided but feel free to use your own to come up with your top (actually bottom) 15 traits. Once you have developed your list of traits, rank them in order of importance to you. Place the trait you dislike the most on line 1, working up in order through line 15. Then, consider how much your partner exhibits that trait. On a scale of 1-5, rate how fully they possess that trait in your opinion based on how often you see that trait.

Sample List: Crudeness, Snoring, No desire to learn or improve, No passion, Burping/farting, Amoral, No filter, No motivation, Lazy, Selfish, Inconsiderate, Controlling, Uneducated, Unfaithful, Critical, Dishonest, Overbearing, Ignorant, Superficial, Unattractive, Lacking sense of humour, Stingy, No/Low Sex Drive, Not physically fit, Unsupportive, Unable to express feelings, Financially insecure, Rude, Mean, Quick to anger, Irresponsible, Unwilling to compromise, Doesn't pull their weight, Oblivious, Snobby

Negative Traits

	Never Exhibits This Trait		Sometimes Exhibits This Trait		Always Exhibits This Trait
Least Desirable Trait: _____	1	2	3	4	5
Trait 2: _____	1	2	3	4	5
Trait 3: _____	1	2	3	4	5
Trait 4: _____	1	2	3	4	5
Trait 5: _____	1	2	3	4	5
Trait 6: _____	1	2	3	4	5
Trait 7: _____	1	2	3	4	5
Trait 8: _____	1	2	3	4	5
Trait 9: _____	1	2	3	4	5

Trait 10: _____	1	2	3	4	5
Trait 11: _____	1	2	3	4	5
Trait 12: _____	1	2	3	4	5
Trait 13: _____	1	2	3	4	5
Trait 14: _____	1	2	3	4	5
Trait 15: _____	1	2	3	4	5

Reflection

You will share your list with your partner in the next exercise, but the ratings are meant for your personal reflection alone. Sharing these scores with your partner could potentially serve only to hurt their feelings without providing you with any benefit.

If you chose to complete this exercise online: We will incorporate this information into your eventual targeted partner chats.

If you chose to complete this exercise in the boxes or on printed pages: You may want to incorporate some of this feedback into your future targeted partner chats. Keep your notes handy, and consider selecting some of these items to discuss when you are selecting your discussion topics.

Split up your positive traits list into essential (items 1-5), important (items 6-10), and nice-to-have (items 11-15). For your essentials list, what are your partner's biggest areas of opportunities (scores of 1-2)? What could they do to improve this score?

Essential Items	What Could Be Done to Improve This Score?
1.	
2.	
3.	
4.	
5.	

Important Items	What Could Be Done to Improve This Score?
1.	
2.	
3.	
4.	
5.	

Nice-to-Have Items	What Could Be Done to Improve This Score?
1.	
2.	
3.	
4.	
5.	

For your negative list, make a note of all of the items in which you scored your partner a 4 or 5. What could they do to improve this score?

Negative Items	What Could Be Done To Improve This Score?
1.	
2.	
3.	
4.	
5.	
6.	
7.	
8.	
9.	
10.	

Ranking Partner Traits

Note: You may choose to complete this exercise one of two ways, depending on how you completed the previous exercise.

1) *If you completed the previous exercise on the website*: Wait until you receive the email response from *Find Fix Forward*. Read the directions below and then go to the link provided in the email to fill out the form. Both partners should complete their own forms separately, and each person will get an individualized email with the information you need for this exercise. *This is the recommended way.*

2) *If you completed the previous exercise in the boxes or on printed pages:* Share the positive and negative partner traits lists you developed in the last exercise with your partner. Provide the lists in random order so that they can rank them in order of perceived importance. Complete the exercise below in the boxes or on printed pages, as with the previous exercises. There will be instructions for what to share with your partner and what to do with the information you receive.

For additional copies of this exercise, visit www.findfixforward.com/resources and click on Exercise 5.

Take the list of personality traits that your partner selected as most important to them and rank them in order of what you think their importance is to your partner. Place the one you think your partner finds most important on line 1 and work your way through in order to line 15. Then, score yourself on how well *you think you meet that need* for your partner. A score of 1 means that you don't feel you possess that trait at all, and a score of 5 means you feel that trait describes you perfectly. Please be very honest in your self-assessment, as this will help greatly while building your program!

Ranking Positive Traits

Ranking Positive Traits

	I Never Exhibit This Trait		I Sometimes Exhibit This Trait		I Always Exhibit This Trait
Most Important Trait: _____	1	2	3	4	5
Trait 2: _____	1	2	3	4	5
Trait 3: _____	1	2	3	4	5
Trait 4: _____	1	2	3	4	5
Trait 5: _____	1	2	3	4	5

Trait 6: _____	1	2	3	4	5
Trait 7: _____	1	2	3	4	5
Trait 8: _____	1	2	3	4	5
Trait 9: _____	1	2	3	4	5
Trait 10: _____	1	2	3	4	5
Trait 11: _____	1	2	3	4	5
Trait 12: _____	1	2	3	4	5
Trait 13: _____	1	2	3	4	5
Trait 14: _____	1	2	3	4	5
Trait 15: _____	1	2	3	4	5

Now, do the same for the negative trait list. Rank the traits in order of which you think your partner desires LEAST (as #1) up through the 15th. As with the positive traits, give yourself a score on how much you possess that trait. A score of 1 means that you do not possess that trait and a score of 5 means that you believe you possess that trait strongly.

Ranking Negative Traits

Ranking Negative Traits

	I Never Exhibit This Trait		I Sometimes Exhibit This Trait		I Always Exhibit This Trait
Least Desirable Trait: _____	1	2	3	4	5
Trait 2: _____	1	2	3	4	5
Trait 3: _____	1	2	3	4	5
Trait 4: _____	1	2	3	4	5
Trait 5: _____	1	2	3	4	5
Trait 6: _____	1	2	3	4	5

Trait 7: _____	1	2	3	4	5
Trait 8: _____	1	2	3	4	5
Trait 9: _____	1	2	3	4	5
Trait 10: _____	1	2	3	4	5
Trait 11: _____	1	2	3	4	5
Trait 12: _____	1	2	3	4	5
Trait 13: _____	1	2	3	4	5
Trait 14: _____	1	2	3	4	5
Trait 15: _____	1	2	3	4	5

Team Share

If you chose to complete this exercise online: Your scores will be compiled and used to help cultivate the most useful partner chats for you to engage in later on. There is no need to share anything with your partner at this time.

If you chose to complete this exercise in the boxes or on printed pages: Once you are finished, share your ranked list and self-assessment scores with your partner. They will share their list and self-assessment with you as well. Remember, you will still not be sharing your assessment of them and they will not be sharing their assessment of you. ONLY share your **self-assessments** based on THEIR positive and negative lists. Your reflections will be based only on how you scored your partner and how they scores themselves, not on how they scored you.

Reflection

Of the positive traits your partner desires, which ones did you give yourself a low score on (scores of 1 or 2)? What actions can you take to improve that score?

Positive Items	What Could Be Done To Improve This Score?
1.	
2.	
3.	
4.	
5.	
6.	
7.	
8.	
9.	
10.	

Of the negative traits your partner does not want in a partner, which ones did you give yourself a high score on (scores of 4 or 5)? What actions can you take (or stop) to improve that score?

Negative Items	What Could Be Done To Improve This Score?
1.	
2.	
3.	
4.	
5.	
6.	
7.	
8.	

9.

10.

If you chose to complete this exercise in the boxes or on printed pages: Now, take a look at your partner's self-assessment and compare it to your own. Jot down any areas of interest. Specifically:

• Were there strong discrepancies in your ranking of importance? For example, they ranked the trait you said was most important to you as a much lower number. A strong rating discrepancy would be anything over a 2 point difference.

_____

_____

_____

_____

_____

_____

• Were there strong discrepancies in your rating of your partner and how they rated themselves for a specific item? A strong rating discrepancy would be anything over a 2 point difference.

_____

_____

_____

_____

_____

_____

You may want to use some of these items for your targeted partner chat topics later, so keep it in a place you will be able to access it at that time.

Our Roles

The roles we expect to play in our relationships don't always end up matching reality. This can be due to circumstances out of our control that get in the way or the personalities of the people involved, but this is often due to the simple fact that not many people sit down and discuss it! One partner may expect to take on the roles surrounding maintaining the household while the other supports the relationship financially, but the other partner may have full expectations to contribute 50/50 to all tasks. This could lead to one or both partners feeling unfulfilled or unappreciated in their contribution to the relationship. We often fall into the roles we expect to play and get annoyed at our partners for not playing the role we expect them to play without ever knowing what role *they* expected to play. No matter what your role ends up being, the important part is that you understand and accept your responsibility in playing that role. When both partners agree on the expectations for each partner in the relationship, there is less room for unhealthy assumptions. Furthermore, a partner not fulfilling their role can be addressed clearly and objectively.

Now, we will take the first step in determining clear, agreed-upon roles for your relationship. For each topic, indicate from 1-9 the amount each task is your responsibility or your partner's. 1 means you are the only one responsible for that task, while 9 means that your partner is the only one responsible for that task. If you complete the task 80% of the time and your partner completes it 20% of the time, select 2. If you share the task equally, select option 5. If you do not currently share some of these duties, indicate what your ideal distribution will be when the time comes to share these responsibilities. After you have scored each option, indicate whether the current distribution of the task is satisfactory to you. There are 10 pre-populated tasks in the first box, with space for an additional 10 of your own creation in the second box if you need. For the items you select as "no," write what your preferred split would be on the lines below the exercise.

For additional copies of this exercise, visit www.findfixforward.com/resources and click on Exercise 6.

Fill-in your own tasks, if applicable:

This is entirely my responsibility			We share this responsibility equally			This is entirely my partner's responsibility			I am satisfied with this distribution of responsibility in this task
1	2	3	4	5	6	7	8	9	

1. Cooking

1	2	3	4	5	6	7	8	9	Yes No

2. Dishes

1	2	3	4	5	6	7	8	9	Yes No

3. Laundry

1	2	3	4	5	6	7	8	9	Yes No

4. Initiating Intimacy

1	2	3	4	5	6	7	8	9	Yes No

5. Parenting Tasks

1	2	3	4	5	6	7	8	9	Yes No

6. Contributing Financially

1	2	3	4	5	6	7	8	9	Yes No

7. Paying bills/household management

1	2	3	4	5	6	7	8	9	Yes No

8. Trip/date planning

1	2	3	4	5	6	7	8	9	Yes No

9. Cleaning

1	2	3	4	5	6	7	8	9	Yes No

10. Outdoor work (lawn, garden, etc.)

1	2	3	4	5	6	7	8	9	Yes No

Fill-in your own tasks, if applicable:

This is entirely my responsibility			We share this responsibility equally			This is entirely my partner's responsibility			I am satisfied with this distribution of responsibility in this task
①	②	③	④	⑤	⑥	⑦	⑧	⑨	

1.

①	②	③	④	⑤	⑥	⑦	⑧	⑨	Yes No

2.

①	②	③	④	⑤	⑥	⑦	⑧	⑨	Yes No

3.

①	②	③	④	⑤	⑥	⑦	⑧	⑨	Yes No

4.

①	②	③	④	⑤	⑥	⑦	⑧	⑨	Yes No

5.

①	②	③	④	⑤	⑥	⑦	⑧	⑨	Yes No

6.

①	②	③	④	⑤	⑥	⑦	⑧	⑨	Yes No

7.

①	②	③	④	⑤	⑥	⑦	⑧	⑨	Yes No

8.

①	②	③	④	⑤	⑥	⑦	⑧	⑨	Yes No

9.

①	②	③	④	⑤	⑥	⑦	⑧	⑨	Yes No

10.

①	②	③	④	⑤	⑥	⑦	⑧	⑨	Yes No

Tasks in which your current distribution is not your ideal:

Task: _____
Preferred changes to be made:

_____

_____

Task: _____
Preferred changes to be made:

_____

_____

Task: _____
Preferred changes to be made:

_____

_____

Task: _____
Preferred changes to be made:

_____

_____

_____

Task: _____
Preferred changes to be made:

_____

_____

_____

Team Share

Once you have both completed your charts, share them and compare. Each partner should take turns listing off an item and sharing what they wrote for the distribution of responsibility for that task, then the other partner should share theirs. For fill-in items your partner wrote, try to come up with the current situation in your mind and share it. After each task, both partners should indicate whether or not the current arrangement is ideal for them. If there are any tasks that one partner responds "no" to, they should indicate the preferred changes to be made. After this conversation, you will both have time to reflect and make a plan for how to best agree on each of the task distributions.

Reflection

On the lines below, reflect on the following questions:
• Were you surprised at how your partner viewed any of your current task distributions? What surprised you?

_____

_____

_____

_____

_____

• Why do you think there was disagreement for these items?

_____

_____

_____

_____

_____

• Are there any areas in which you disagree about how the tasks are currently being split and completed? Which ones?

_____

_____

_____

_____

_____

• For those items, how do you propose a more mutually satisfactory arrangement?

_____

_____

_____

_____

_____

_____

_____

_____

_____

Forward Focus

Check in with each other regularly to make sure the distribution still works for both of you. Life often gets in the way and things change, so be flexible and ready to shift tasks either in the short or long term.

Couple spotlight: Maria and Andy rotate some of their tasks each month so that they don't get bored with the monotony of completing the same tasks over and over. This allows both of them to feel they are contributing equally and that they are supported.

How We Give and Receive Affection

Not all affection is created equal, and not everyone likes the same type. We all have specific ways of showing affection or appreciation that feel the best to us. Some people feel appreciated most when their partner comes home with flowers, while others need to hear words of affirmation. The problem comes in when one partner feels appreciated most when their partner does nice things for them, but their partner spends a ton of money and energy showering them with expensive gifts. Perhaps that partner personally feels most appreciated when they are given gifts to show their partner's love and appreciation, but they are operating on an assumption that everyone feels the same way. This can often lead to people feeling underappreciated, even when the exact opposite is true! Getting to the root of how to best make your partner *feel* your appreciation (not just how to *show* them from your perspective) will help you to avoid unnecessary stress and worry.

Let's get to the root of your appreciation style. On the lines below or on your printed sheets, write down examples of what you do to make sure your partner feels appreciated. How do you show affection? These could be little things, like sending texts throughout the day to check on them, or bigger things like planning surprise dates or trips for them. Next, explain why you do those things. What do you think these actions say to your partner? When you do them, how do they respond? Do they respond as you hoped they would, or does it seem like they don't understand your intent? They may not even react at all or notice that you've done something. Finally, consider the things you would like your partner to do to show you appreciation and affection. These can be things they are already doing that make you feel appreciated, or they can be things that are not currently done. What would these actions say to you?

For additional copies of this exercise, visit www.findfixforward.com/resources and click on Exercise 7.

1) What do you do to make your partner feel appreciated?

_____

_____

_____

_____

2) What do you think these actions say to them?

_____

_____

_____

_____

3) How do they react?

_____

_____

_____

_____

4) What things would you like your partner to do to show you appreciation/affection?

_____

_____

_____

_____

_____

5) What would these actions say to you?

_____

_____

_____

_____

_____

Team Share

Once you have both determined your current mode of showing affection and appreciation to your partner and your desired method of receiving it back, share your reflections. This session can follow the exact structure of the exercise questions, with each partner sharing items 1-5 in order. Remember, you should use this as an opportunity to simply listen and try to understand your partner here, especially if what they share is contrary to what you expected to hear.

Reflection

After your sharing session, consider the following questions.

1) Did my partner share anything during this session that surprised me? What was it?

_____

_____

_____

2) Have you been on the same page with this topic, understanding what each partner needed?

     Yes   No

3) In what ways can I modify my behaviour to ensure that my partner feels appreciated and loved *in the way they prefer to be*?

_____

_____

_____

_____

_____

Forward Focus

Make a plan for doing one thing each day to show your partner how much you appreciate them.

Couple spotlight: Elizabeth and Derrick end their day by sharing one thing they are grateful for in regard to their partner that day. This allows them to constantly re-focus on the positives of their relationship and how much they value each other.

How We Give and Receive Feedback

Most of us are bad at giving feedback. We don't think carefully enough about our wording, the environment, the circumstances the other person is going through, or the tone we choose. Worst of all, we often give the feedback during a fight and it comes out as an attack because we don't think it through before saying (or yelling it) at our partner. On the other hand, most of us are even worse at receiving feedback. We feel like our partner is directly attacking us, being unfair, or refusing to see our true intentions behind the actions, and this is especially true in the middle of a fight. We need to get over ourselves (and be kinder to ourselves) and realize that this is for our own good, let alone our partner's own good! It's important to remember that one of the most valuable roles our partners (and our bosses, family members, friends, etc.) play in our lives is to help us to become better people. Feedback is a gift, even though it may not feel like it in the moment. Just as children learn how to behave with siblings and friends during childhood, we learn through our experiences with these important people in our lives how to be more successful as a partner, employee, family member, and friend. If we go into a relationship thinking that we have no growing or improving to do, we are setting ourselves up for an unsatisfying relationship on both sides. Similarly, if we only provide feedback during an argument, we are never going to be successful in getting our point across and actually achieving our goal of being heard and helping to improve our partner and our relationship. Feedback doesn't have to feel like a blame game, although we often automatically take it that way.

Everyone has a different communication style, and that's okay. The key is understanding our partner's communication style and doing our best to communicate with them in the way that allows them to best *hear and receive our message.* Having different communication styles does not make you a bad match, but it certainly can if you don't learn how your partner prefers to be communicated with — especially when the news isn't good. Learning how your partner prefers to receive feedback is the first step to effective communication, but you may not even have a firm grasp on the way *you* prefer to receive feedback yet. Consider the following statements, and check the boxes next to the ones that feel the most true for you:

For additional copies of this exercise, visit www.findfixforward.com/resources and click on Exercise 8.

How do you prefer to receive feedback?

Select as many as you want.

When receiving feedback from my partner, I want them to be direct and just say what they are feeling and how I can fix it.

I need my partner to use a softer approach, padding the feedback and reassuring me that they still love me.

After receiving feedback, I need to be able to discuss it immediately and take action.

After receiving feedback, I need some time to myself to think before I know exactly how I want to respond or react.

Reassurances from my partner before/after being given

feedback make me feel like they are being patronizing.

Reassurances from my partner before/after being given feedback makes me feel safe and more able to receive the feedback.

I need my partner to tell me exactly what they want me to do to fix it so I don't waste time coming up with solutions that will not help the situation.

I need to be given a lot of clarity — give me examples so that I can put my finger on exact times that are being referred to and make the connections.

I don't need examples — the fact that I've made my partner feel a certain way is enough and defending specific circumstances isn't relevant.

Team Share

Once you both have a clearer understanding of how you prefer to receive feedback, share those statements with your partner. Read the statements out loud, elaborating if necessary to more fully explain what would benefit you the most. Now, give it a try! Use something completely ridiculous to give your partner feedback on, and make sure to use the style in which they feel most comfortable. For example, use something like "it really bothers me that you like the colour green." Have fun with it, but start getting more comfortable with how best to communicate with your partner to express your feelings effectively.

Reflection

Consider what you learned from your partner. Is your current method working to help them improve, or do you need to modify how you approach situations involving feedback or criticism? What can you commit to starting, stopping, or changing to be most helpful?

_____
_____
_____
_____
_____
_____

Forward Focus

Shed the fear of giving and receiving feedback! Request feedback more regularly from your partner and genuinely take their words to heart.

Couple spotlight: Daniella and Mario ask each other "can I be a mirror for a second?" or "can you be a mirror for me?" This allows them to provide or receive feedback from their partner on something that may be sensitive but comes across as helpful and not accusatory.

Bonus Forward Focus!

Consider: What do we stand to gain?

Before giving feedback, think how much your relationship stands to gain from bringing it to your partner's attention. Is it something petty that you could easily let go, or will there be a genuine benefit to your relationship? If it's easy to let go, let it go.

The Root of The Problem

The things that bother us about our partners are almost never the actual problems in our relationships. They are symptoms, stirring up negative emotions while covering up what actually needs to be addressed. We often confuse these symptoms for problems, since they are easier to work on. If it drives you nuts that your partner snores, you can look into therapeutic treatments or medicines to help, but consider this: when you were first falling in love with your partner, did their snoring bother you? Probably not. You might have even thought it was cute. Maybe it was something you were less than excited about, but you likely didn't spend the night gritting your teeth and wanting to hold a pillow over their face to get the noise to stop. The same often goes for negative actions within a relationship, like when a partner lies, yells, insults, or even cheats. These are also symptoms. Under each symptom, you will find a root if you look hard enough. The important thing is to get to the root of the problem and stop just trying to correct the symptoms.

Let's try to identify the roots of issues in your relationship. On the lines below or on your printed page, jot down all of the things that frustrate you about your partner. These can be physical things, like the way they wear their hair or the clothes they choose. They can be actions, like how they choose to spend their money or their time, how they load the dishwasher, or how they parent. They can also be the way they interact with you or members of your family or friends. They can be as petty or as meaningful as you want. Use a new line for each item. After you have listed all of them, indicate if each item is a symptom or the root of the problem. Once you've done that, for all of the symptoms you identified, try to come up with the root of the issue. The root could be why you think your partner does a specific thing that bothers you, or it could be why that thing bothers you. There are a lot of things our partners do unconsciously, so the question may need to be more inwardly based to determine what that action makes you feel.

For additional copies of this exercise, visit www.findfixforward.com/resources and click on Exercise 9.

1) What is the action that frustrates you?

2) Is this a symptom of a deeper issue or the root?

3) If it is a symptom, what do you think the real root may be?

This is just a hypothesis, but really try to dig deep to look well below the surface. One way to get to the root is by the "why times 5" exercise. Ask yourself why it bothers you, then take that answer and ask it again until you've asked 5 times. This may help you to get closer to the root and stop thinking about superficial issues.

Frustrating Behavior	Symptom or Root?	Hypothesized Real Root

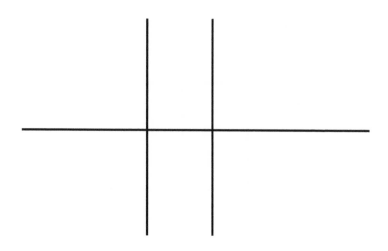

Reflection

This is an individual exercise for your personal reflection and development in considering how get past the things that frustrate you. Now, for all of the items you listed as symptoms: take a deep breath, then find a way to LET THEM GO. Addressing the roots of problems is an important exercise in order to relieve future issues caused by the same problem, but continuing to fight over how your partner loads the dishwasher isn't benefitting either of you.

Also, keep in mind that your list of things that bother you will continue to grow and change over time. This week it may be the dishwasher, but next week (depending on what's going on with you personally or the relationship as a whole) it could be the laundry, the way they drive, or any other little thing that arises. Find a way to incorporate the "root or symptom" question into your regular way of thinking to make this a constant reflection that allows you to stop "sweating the small stuff" and focus on just enjoying your relationship.

Forward Focus

Use the "so what?" rule.

Couple spotlight: When Kristy notices something about Jerrod that bothers her, she asks herself "so what?" so that she can have an honest conversation with herself about how much it affects her and/or their relationship. "I don't like the way Jerrod loads the dishwasher. So what? If the dishes are still getting done, why does it matter to me how he does it if it's working for him? Also, I should use this opportunity to show my gratitude to him for doing them in the first place!"

Remember, your role is to support your partner's development, not to change them to fit your image. Learning to let go of the things that don't matter will give you an immense amount of freedom and relieve a ton of stress!

What We Hold Onto

Over time, it is (unfortunately) natural for couples to develop resentment. It is normal for us to hold on to things, sweep things under the rug, and silently stew over words and actions that hurt us because we don't feel like making an issue about them at the time. Maybe things are already stressful and we don't want to make them worse, or things are going well and we don't want to ruin it with a complaint. Maybe we tried giving feedback in the past that wasn't received well, and it has made us shy to try again. If these issues don't eventually blow up into an argument, they are likely serving to harden us and to make us less forgiving in the future. This often results in us wanting to scream when our partner chews loudly instead of being able to blissfully ignore it, and often causes problems that never truly needed to be problems.

Another thing we may be holding on to might be an unfulfilled life goal. Sometimes we get bogged down by unfulfilled wishes and hopes, whether or not we realize it. Over time, we may experience more and more examples of the things we wanted for our lives slipping away. This doesn't necessarily have to be a negative thing, however — some of our hopes and dreams change over time as we mature or our focus shifts. Occasionally, though, a decision is made or an event occurs that makes something we previously wished for impossible to achieve. You may have always hoped to raise your children near their cousins, only to find your spouse's job causing you to move across the country. You may have wanted to be a stay-at-home mom, but the household income couldn't support it and you had to go back to work. Whatever the situation and whatever the reason it went unfulfilled, resentment and blame can begin to build. Over time, without even realizing it, you may begin to resent your partner for these unfulfilled desires. In order to move forward, we need to first identify and acknowledge the loss. Then, we need to find a way to let it go once and for all.

During the upcoming exercises, we are going to be getting ready to share a lot of feedback. This may feel uncomfortable, but the goal is for you to find a safe space together to truly hear each other and reflect on how your partner is feeling about each of the topics discussed. You have already learned how your partner prefers to receive feedback, so keep that in mind as we move forward. As you begin these exercises, try to adopt a growth mindset and put down your barriers. The first step in doing this is to figure out what is getting in the way of your relationship. Consider what you are holding onto, whether consciously or subconsciously. This may mean an unresolved issue from the past, an issue that you never discussed at all, a way you were made to feel by your partner, or even a small action that you were able to shrug off at the time. Take some time to really be honest with yourself about what is still in there, niggling at you from the dark recesses of your brain, whether you think about it regularly or never. Here are a few examples:

My partner cheated on me in the past. Although we worked through that issue a long time ago, it's always something that affects my behaviour even though we don't talk about it.

We got into a fight when we were drinking, and my partner said something really hurtful to me. They said they didn't mean it, but I've become insecure about it since then.

The way my partner interacts with other people I think they find attractive makes me anxious.

The way my partner interacts with my family and friends makes me feel like they don't care about or like them.

I had an experience with a previous ex that I think may be affecting the way I treat my current partner.

I caught my partner in a lie once and I can't be sure I can trust them all of the time.

I wanted to have children at an early age, but my partner didn't want that.

I worry that my partner gave up a lot to be with me and that I will never be enough.

In the box below or on your printed page, create a list of the things you hold onto that may be affecting your relationship. Then, for each item, write what would have to happen in order for you to let it go. It may need to be a conversation, it may need to be your partner stopping or starting something, or it may be more complicated than that. You may simply need to acknowledge and mourn the loss. For the life goals that went unfulfilled, identify who (or what) you are blaming for the loss. This is just the beginning of the conversation, so don't worry if you are unsure how to move forward.

Example: My partner was unfaithful. In order to let it go, I feel I need to hear all of the details because I still have a lot of uncertainty about what happened and why.

For additional copies of this exercise, visit www.findfixforward.com/resources and click on Exercise 10.

Thing You Are Holding Onto	Who/What Are You Blaming?	What needs to happen for you to let it go?

Team Share

This one takes courage and vulnerability, but the process of uprooting the barriers that are holding you back can be incredibly powerful and healing for you as an individual and for you as a couple. Share the items you listed and your thoughts on what would need to happen for you to be able to let them go and stop letting them affect your present.

Reflection
After your sharing session, consider the following questions:
    1) How did sharing those details feel?

_____
_____
_____
_____
_____

2) Do you feel that you have relieved any of the pressure by simply telling your partner you were holding on to some of the items?

_____

_____

_____

_____

_____

3) Did anything your partner shared surprise you?

_____

_____

_____

_____

_____

4) Do you have any suggestions for how you can help your partner let go of any of their concerns that they didn't already suggest?

_____

_____

_____

_____

_____

How We React

Everyone acts differently when they get upset, overwhelmed, or hurt. Everyone needs something a little bit different than the next person, and that's okay. The issue comes in when we assume that everyone else should handle things the way we handle them and we don't give others what *they* need. You may not have spent a lot of time thinking about how your behaviours change when your mood changes, but your partner could probably give you a lesson in this. We are much more sensitive to changes in the behaviours of our partners because they trigger worry in us, but we don't notice the small changes in ourselves. The first thing we need to do is to understand ourselves. Why do we instinctively do the things we do, often not even being aware that we are doing them? When we understand how and why we react the way we do, we can make progress towards either changing the negative behaviour or expressing more clearly to our partner what we need.

This exercise focuses on how you respond and your perception of your partner's response to certain situations. Below is a list of situations that often cause negative emotional or physical responses. First, select three of these that you feel you may respond to in an unhealthy or unhelpful way. For each situation, describe how you react, then explain why you act that way (or what you get out of responding that way). Finally, write down how you **would like to** react in that situation.

Once you have filled out the section about your reactions, do the same for your partner. Determine the three situations in which you think your partner reacts in an unhealthy or unhelpful way. For each situation, describe how they react, then explain why you *think* they act that way (or what they get out of responding that way). Intent is a tricky thing, as our feelings about why they do the things they do may be very different from the reality in their heads. It may feel like our partner wants us to feel badly or be punished, but they may just be reacting in the way that feels most comfortable for them without even considering how it affects you. Finally, write down how you **would like them to** react in that situation.

For additional copies of this exercise, visit www.findfixforward.com/resources and click on Exercise 11.

Example situations: you feel overwhelmed, you are stressed, you are sad, your partner did something to upset you, you are angry, you received bad news, you are embarrassed, you are anxious, you feel "meh," you are bored, you are worried, you are scared, you are challenged, you are feeling insecure, you are confused.

Feel free to add your own situations that aren't listed here.

	Stimulus 1:	Stimulus 2:	Stimulus 3:
How Do You React? *Explain the actions you take. Do you yell, shut down, cry, say mean things, get petty, use sarcasm, or hide?*			
Why Do You React This Way? *What do you get out of reacting this way? Does it make you feel better at the time, or give you back some power you feel you lost? Do you need time to think, or*			

respond without thinking?			
How Would You Ideally Like To React?			
If emotions were not involved and you could be completely level-headed, how would you like to respond so that you have the best outcome?			

<u>Now do this exercise for each of your partner's 3 situations</u>
1) Your partner's stimulus?
2) How do they react?
3) Why do you think they react this way?
4) How would you ideally like them to react?

	Stimulus 1:	*Stimulus 2:*	*Stimulus 3:*
How Do They React?			
Why Do You Think They React This Way?			

*How Would
You Ideally
Like Them
To React?*

Team Share

Once you have both completed this exercise, take the opportunity to share what you wrote. Try to utilize this structure:

When ____(your stimulus happens)_____, I realize that I often _____(how you react)_____. I do this because _____(why you react this way)_____, but I know I would get a better outcome if I were able to _____(how you would prefer to react)_____.

Example: When you criticize the way I do something, I realize that I often get defensive and shut down instead of listening and trying to understand. I do this because my feelings get hurt and I feel misunderstood, especially when I think my way of doing it is right, but I know I would get a better outcome if I were able to just listen and reflect on what you say and how we could both benefit from doing it another way.

After each partner shares all 3 of their personal situations, share your thoughts on your partner's reactions. Try to utilize this structure:

When ____(their stimulus happens)_____, you often _____(how they react)_____. I think you do this because _____(why you think they react that way)_____, but I believe we would get a better outcome if you were able to _____(how you would prefer them to react)_____.

93

Finally, work together to come up with a compromise response that works for both partners. For each situation, consider the way you both currently respond, the way you wish you responded, and the way your partner wishes you responded. Then, come up with a reaction that will help you to meet somewhere in the middle and make you both feel comfortable.

You won't always be able to stick to this plan perfectly since emotions have a tendency of taking over in high-stress situations, but having an action plan for how you WANT to react (in a way that works for both of you) will help to avoid huge blow-ups and unnecessary worry or hurt. Try your best to keep this plan in mind when the situations arise, and don't be afraid to remind your partner (gently) of what you agreed to if they revert back to their instinctual behaviours.

Reflection

Use the box below to write down your action plan for how you agreed you would like to respond to your trigger situations. Refer back to it often, and reflect on how well you have been able to stick to your plan when the situations arise.

Stimulus	How You Would Like To React	How Your Partner Would Like You To React

Stimulus 1:

Agreed-Upon Modified Reaction:

Stimulus 2:

Agreed-Upon Modified Reaction:

Stimulus 3:

Agreed-Upon Modified Reaction:

Intention and Empathy

Having our intent frequently misjudged by our partner can be incredibly damaging. It can cause us to question ourselves, how our partner sees us as a person and a partner, and can cause anxiety that leads to further suspicion, misunderstanding, and anger. Unfortunately, we often judge ourselves by our intentions and others by their actions. We read between the lines, looking for ulterior motives and hidden meanings. We make assumptions about why our partners do or say things based on our perspective and interpretation of the situation, and we don't always take the time to try to see things through their eyes. More often than not, these interpretations are negative. "Is that what you're wearing tonight?" can go quickly from an intention of "are you ready to go or do you need more time?" to "you look awful in that, I can't believe you are wearing that." These misinterpreted assumptions about intention can lead to two things, and neither of them are good. They can lead to a fight right then and there, or they can lead to resentment being built up and feelings being hurt silently. This can also lead to the partner being more sensitive to clues that support the assumption, no matter how untrue they are.

Being truly empathetic to your partner means trying to see things from their perspective. It means thinking about how your actions, no matter how good the intent behind them, may come across and affect them. It means checking in when their mood seems to have changed to see if something happened that they haven't yet shared with you.

Intention and empathy are deeply connected, as being empathetic to your partner's feelings will allow you to more clearly see their true intentions. Being empathetic to your partner's feelings will also allow you to communicate with them more effectively, as you can put yourself in their shoes and understand how your actions and statements may make them feel. It will minimize misunderstandings and allow you to cut through the worries, doubts, and frustrations that we often create for ourselves without realizing it.

Think about a time when your partner said something relatively routine that you took in a negative way. What did they say, and how did you interpret it? Why do you think you interpreted it that way? Is there a history of your partner using passive-aggressive tactics to try to manipulate your behaviour, or do they regularly treat you with respect and care? Was it something about your mood or attitude towards your partner that caused you to immediately assume the worst, or was it something about the way they said it? On the lines below or on your printed page, take some time to come up with a few situations from your history that you may have misjudged and analyse them. There is room for three examples, but feel free to print more pages if you need them. The goal is not necessarily to analyse each situation in a vacuum, but to rather look for and identify trends in the way our personal feelings and insecurities may affect the way we perceive our partner's words and actions.

For additional copies of this exercise, visit www.findfixforward.com/resources and click on Exercise 12.

Example 1:

1. What was said?

For each event you recall, try to remember what was actually said.

_____

_____

_____

2. How was it said?

Was there a tone used that caused you to interpret it in a negative way, or was it more about the words chosen? Was the situation around the comment negative?

_____

_____

_____

3. How did you interpret it?

What did you interpret the statement to mean?

_____

_____

_____

4. Why did you interpret it this way?

Why do you think you interpreted it this way? Was it internal or external?

_____

_____

_____

5. What happened after?

Did you change your behaviour, start an argument, or just hold on to the hurt feelings? How did your interpretation cause you to act towards your partner?

_____

_____

_____

6. How did your partner respond?

Were they confused, not understanding why you were upset?

_____

_____

_____

Example 2:

1. What was said?

For each event you recall, try to remember what was actually said.

_____

_____

_____

2. How was it said?

Was there a tone used that caused you to interpret it in a negative way, or was it more about the words chosen? Was the situation around the comment negative?

_____

_____

_____

3. How did you interpret it?

What did you interpret the statement to mean?

_____

_____

_____

4. Why did you interpret it this way?

Why do you think you interpreted it this way? Was it internal or external?

_____

_____

_____

5. What happened after?

Did you change your behaviour, start an argument, or just hold on to the hurt feelings? How did your interpretation cause you to act towards your partner?

_____

_____

_____

6. How did your partner respond?

Were they confused, not understanding why you were upset?

_____

_____

_____

Example 3:

1. What was said?

For each event you recall, try to remember what was actually said.

_____

_____

_____

2. How was it said?

Was there a tone used that caused you to interpret it in a negative way, or was it more about the words chosen? Was the situation around the comment negative?

_____

_____

_____

3. How did you interpret it?

What did you interpret the statement to mean?

_____

4. Why did you interpret it this way?

Why do you think you interpreted it this way? Was it internal or external?

_____

_____

_____

5. What happened after?

Did you change your behaviour, start an argument, or just hold on to the hurt feelings? How did your interpretation cause you to act towards your partner?

_____

_____

_____

6. How did your partner respond?

Were they confused, not understanding why you were upset?

_____

_____

_____

Forward Focus

The best piece of advice I have for avoiding unnecessary drama, hurt feelings, and fights in any relationship is to always assume good intent. Ask yourself if a bystander in the room would have interpreted the statement that way. If they wouldn't, you may be putting a spin on the statement that was not intended and may be causing you unnecessary worry and hurt feelings. If that doesn't work, ask for clarification. A simple request for more information about what they said or why they were asking the question can go a long way to cut through the noise and avoid an argument that no one wanted to have.

Identifying Statements

This is your final exercise before the team sharing sessions! Congratulations on putting in such hard work throughout this program!

Note: You may choose to complete this exercise one of two ways.

1) Go to www.findfixforward.com/statements to fill out your form. Both partners should complete their form separately, and the information will be used to begin building your final program. If you choose to complete this exercise this way, we will analyse your answers and provide you with a customized discussion list, thus keeping your scores private but allowing for more purposeful conversations. Discussion topics will be chosen based on 3 criteria:

• Positive responses from both partners (to celebrate the successes in your relationship).

• Negative responses from both partners (to allow you to talk through issues that you both agree may need some improvement).

• Answers that do not agree (where one partner's perceptive of the situation is significantly more positive or negative than the other's, and this discrepancy should be addressed).

This is the recommended way and will achieve the

greatest results. You can choose to do this exercise on the portal even if you did not complete previous exercises on the portal.

2) Complete the exercise below in the box or on printed pages, as with the previous exercises. The information you write should be kept private, as it is meant for personal reflection unless otherwise indicated. If you choose to complete this exercise this way, each partner should select five topics to start that have very high positive scores and five topics with very negative scores to discuss in the next exercise. If you feel you have more than five that are worth discussing, feel free to add more on when you are finished with the first round.

*This method doesn't allow for discussions based on discrepancies in scores.

For additional copies of this exercise, visit www.findfixforward.com/resources and click on Exercise 13.

In your relationship, how often/much do you feel the following statements apply to you?

	Strongly Agree	Agree	Neither	Disagree	Strongly Disagree
My partner pays attention to me and truly listens to what I care about.	1	2	3	4	5
My partner knows me on a deep level.	1	2	3	4	5
My partner and I are able to argue in a healthy way.	1	2	3	4	5

We have intellectual, stimulating conversations.	*1*	*2*	*3*	*4*	*5*
I feel that my partner and I are equals.	*1*	*2*	*3*	*4*	*5*
I make my partner laugh regularly.	*1*	*2*	*3*	*4*	*5*
My partner makes me laugh regularly.	*1*	*2*	*3*	*4*	*5*

My partner and I find the same things funny.	1	2	3	4	5
I am my partner's 1st priority.	1	2	3	4	5
My partner does little things for me to make me feel special.	1	2	3	4	5
My partner supports the things I want to do.	1	2	3	4	5

I feel desired by my partner.	1	2	3	4	5
I feel desire for my partner.	1	2	3	4	5
I have fun with my partner when it is just the two of us.	1	2	3	4	5
I want to spend more time with my partner as a couple.	1	2	3	4	5

My partner and I act as teammates and conquer all of our problems together.	*1*	*2*	*3*	*4*	*5*
I don't feel judged by my partner.	*1*	*2*	*3*	*4*	*5*
My partner cares about my career.	*1*	*2*	*3*	*4*	*5*
My partner loves my family and friends as their own.	*1*	*2*	*3*	*4*	*5*

I love my partner's family and friends as my own.	1	2	3	4	5
My partner satisfies all of my needs in the bedroom.	1	2	3	4	5
I think I satisfy all of my partner's needs in the bedroom.	1	2	3	4	5
My partner and I have a lot of passion for each other.	1	2	3	4	5

It is important that I go to sleep with my partner in the bed next to me at night.	*1*	*2*	*3*	*4*	*5*
I think it is important for my partner to have me in bed next to them at night.	*1*	*2*	*3*	*4*	*5*
I look forward to seeing my partner every day.	*1*	*2*	*3*	*4*	*5*
I think my partner looks forward to seeing me every day.	*1*	*2*	*3*	*4*	*5*

When I'm not with my partner, I miss them.	1	2	3	4	5
I can talk to my partner about anything.	1	2	3	4	5
My partner can talk to me about anything.	1	2	3	4	5
I spend a lot of energy trying to change my partner.	1	2	3	4	5

My partner tries to change things about me.	*1*	*2*	*3*	*4*	*5*
My partner shares their concerns with me without worry.	*1*	*2*	*3*	*4*	*5*
I am comfortable sharing my concerns with my partner.	*1*	*2*	*3*	*4*	*5*
I enjoy time away from my partner.	*1*	*2*	*3*	*4*	*5*

I have no secrets from my partner.	1	2	3	4	5
I don't think my partner has any secrets from me.	1	2	3	4	5
I spend a lot of time thinking about what my partner may be hiding from me.	1	2	3	4	5
I feel that I put more into our relationship than my partner does.	1	2	3	4	5

I feel that we have an equal distribution of household responsibilities.	1	2	3	4	5
If my relationship ended, I feel that I would move on and have a happy life.	1	2	3	4	5
If my relationship ended, I feel that my partner would move on and have a happy life.	1	2	3	4	5
My partner understands and appreciates the sacrifices I make for them.	1	2	3	4	5

I have a lot of interests outside of my relationship.	*1*	*2*	*3*	*4*	*5*
My partner makes me feel desired and attractive.	*1*	*2*	*3*	*4*	*5*
I understand what turns my partner on.	*1*	*2*	*3*	*4*	*5*
My partner understands what turns me on.	*1*	*2*	*3*	*4*	*5*

I feel comfortable expressing my feelings.	*1*	*2*	*3*	*4*	*5*
I worry about how my partner will accept criticism if I were to express it.	*1*	*2*	*3*	*4*	*5*
My partner and I share the same interests.	*1*	*2*	*3*	*4*	*5*
If I have an instinct about how someone is feeling, I'm usually correct.	*1*	*2*	*3*	*4*	*5*

My partner and I both know what makes each other feel appreciated individually and do it regularly.	*1*	*2*	*3*	*4*	*5*
In long term relationships, the practical aspects of a partnership are more important than romance.	*1*	*2*	*3*	*4*	*5*
My partner would never do anything that they wouldn't share with me.	*1*	*2*	*3*	*4*	*5*
I often reflect on how me and my actions are perceived by others.	*1*	*2*	*3*	*4*	*5*

I'm getting what I expect out of this relationship.	*1*	*2*	*3*	*4*	*5*
I think my partner is getting what they want out of this relationship.	*1*	*2*	*3*	*4*	*5*
I think my partner and I have the same idea of what an ideal relationship should be.	*1*	*2*	*3*	*4*	*5*
I worry that we will not be able to agree on a mutually beneficial plan for fixing our relationship.	*1*	*2*	*3*	*4*	*5*

I feel that my partner accepts me for who I am.

1	*2*	*3*	*4*	*5*

Targeted Couple Chats

Now all of the analysis and assessment will really begin to pay off! Some of this may be difficult, but it will be incredibly rewarding and therapeutic for your relationship. Whether or not you completed the last section online, you will complete this series of exercises the same way, only the setup will be different.

If you completed the identifying statements online: For every session in this section, you will receive two topic statements that you rated during the "identifying statements" exercises.

If you completed the identifying statements manually: For every session in this section, each partner should select one topic to discuss. Try to include one positive topic and one negative topic for each session, and share the topics beforehand.

Together, you are going to discuss those topics. Some topics will be good (you both scored the topic well, and it's just nice to share positive feedback with each other), some will be areas for improvement (you both scored the topics low, and things need to be shared/discussed), and some will be areas in which there were large discrepancies in your scoring. Sharing your actual scores is not a recommended part of this exercise, the only thing that matters is that you clearly explain your feelings on the topic.

Before sitting down together, take the time to really think

through what you want to say. Write it down. Write it like a letter, use bullet points, or whatever method best works for you so that you get across everything you need to. Don't hold back, as the most important part of this exercise is to be honest and open about the things that are getting in the way of your relationship.

The format of sharing is up to you, but make sure that you take the time and space to sit down together and share your topics verbally. Feel free to use your notes or even read them aloud to your partner if you are worried you are going to forget something, but do not simply hand each other the notes to read. You with both get more from the exercise if you are able to see how your partner really feels and reacts to both your statements and their own.

The purpose of this exercise is for you to hear and understand each other, not to defend your position. You should not interject while your partner is speaking or attempt to explain why their feelings aren't accurate — your only job is to hear them at this point. If things are difficult to discuss or hear, feel free to pause and walk away for a break. Take turns expressing your position about each of the topics, but do not respond to your partner's portion. After the exercise is complete, you will have the opportunity to reflect by yourself to work through your feelings about what has been shared with you.

For each topic, consider the following points:

1) Explain the current state for this topic in your relationship (e.g. I feel anxious about sharing my concerns with you and end up keeping a lot to myself).

2) What are the observed behaviours that caused you to give the rating you gave? Avoid statements based on presumed intent (do not discuss what you think your partner thought/felt during the experience that caused them to respond that way)

—stick only to the things that happened.

3) Explain what your picture of the ideal state would be for this topic. Give examples of ways you or your partner could get a better score. (e.g. I would like it if you texted me during the day to tell me that you were thinking of me).

10 topic pages are included, but feel free to print more if you need them.

Topic: _____

1. Explain the current state for this topic in your relationship (e.g. I feel anxious about sharing my concerns with you and end up keeping a lot to myself).

_____
_____
_____
_____
_____
_____
_____
_____
_____

2. What are the observed behaviours that caused you to give the rating you gave? Avoid statements based on presumed intent (do not discuss what you think your partner thought/felt during the experience that caused them to respond that way) stick only to the things that happened.

_____
_____
_____
_____
_____
_____

3. Explain what your picture of the ideal state would be for this topic. Give examples of ways you or your partner could get a better score. (e.g. I would like it if you texted me during the day to tell me that you were thinking of me).

_____

_____

_____

_____

_____

_____

_____

_____

_____

_____

Topic: _____

1. Explain the current state for this topic in your relationship (e.g. I feel anxious about sharing my concerns with you and end up keeping a lot to myself).

_____

_____

_____

_____

_____

_____

_____

2. What are the observed behaviours that caused you to give the rating you gave? Avoid statements based on presumed intent (do not discuss what you think your partner thought/felt during the experience that caused them to respond that way)-stick only to the things that happened.

_____
_____
_____
_____
_____
_____
_____

3. Explain what your picture of the ideal state would be for this topic. Give examples of ways you or your partner could get a better score. (e.g. I would like it if you texted me during the day to tell me that you were thinking of me).

_____
_____
_____
_____
_____
_____
_____
_____
_____

Topic: _____

1. Explain the current state for this topic in your relationship (e.g. I feel anxious about sharing my concerns with you and end up keeping a lot to myself).

_____
_____
_____
_____
_____
_____
_____

2. What are the observed behaviours that caused you to give the rating you gave? Avoid statements based on presumed intent (do not discuss what you think your partner thought/felt during the experience that caused them to respond that way)-stick only to the things that happened.

_____

_____

_____

_____

_____

_____

3. Explain what your picture of the ideal state would be for this topic. Give examples of ways you or your partner could get a better score. (e.g. I would like it if you texted me during the day to tell me that you were thinking of me).

_____

_____

_____

_____

_____

_____

_____

_____

_____

_____

Topic: _____

1. Explain the current state for this topic in your relationship (e.g. I feel anxious about sharing my concerns with you and end up keeping a lot to myself).

_____

_____

_____

_____

_____

_____

_____

2. What are the observed behaviours that caused you to give the rating you gave? Avoid statements based on presumed intent (do not discuss what you think your partner thought/felt during the experience that caused them to respond that way)- stick only to the things that happened.

_____

_____

_____

_____

_____

_____

_____

3. Explain what your picture of the ideal state would be for this topic. Give examples of ways you or your partner could get a better score. (e.g. I would like it if you texted me during the day to tell me that you were thinking of me).

_____

_____

_____

_____

_____

_____

_____

_____

_____

_____

Topic: _____

1. Explain the current state for this topic in your relationship (e.g. I feel anxious about sharing my concerns with you and end up keeping a lot to myself).

_____
_____
_____
_____
_____
_____

2. What are the observed behaviours that caused you to give the rating you gave? Avoid statements based on presumed intent (do not discuss what you think your partner thought/felt during the experience that caused them to respond that way)-stick only to the things that happened.

_____
_____
_____
_____
_____
_____

3. Explain what your picture of the ideal state would be for this topic. Give examples of ways you or your partner could get a better score. (e.g. I would like it if you texted me during the day to tell me that you were thinking of me).

_____
_____
_____
_____

_____

_____

_____

_____

_____

_____

Topic: _____

1. Explain the current state for this topic in your relationship (e.g. I feel anxious about sharing my concerns with you and end up keeping a lot to myself).

_____

_____

_____

_____

_____

_____

2. What are the observed behaviours that caused you to give the rating you gave? Avoid statements based on presumed intent (do not discuss what you think your partner thought/felt during the experience that caused them to respond that way)- stick only to the things that happened.

_____

_____

_____

_____

_____

_____

3. Explain what your picture of the ideal state would be for this topic. Give examples of ways you or your partner could get a better score. (e.g. I would like it if you texted me

during the day to tell me that you were thinking of me).

_____

_____

_____

_____

_____

_____

_____

_____

_____

Topic: _____

1. Explain the current state for this topic in your relationship (e.g. I feel anxious about sharing my concerns with you and end up keeping a lot to myself).

_____

_____

_____

_____

_____

_____

2. What are the observed behaviours that caused you to give the rating you gave? Avoid statements based on presumed intent (do not discuss what you think your partner thought/felt during the experience that caused them to respond that way)- stick only to the things that happened.

_____

_____

_____

_____

_____

_____

_____

3. Explain what your picture of the ideal state would be for this topic. Give examples of ways you or your partner could get a better score. (e.g. I would like it if you texted me during the day to tell me that you were thinking of me).

_____

_____

_____

_____

_____

_____

_____

_____

_____

Topic: _____

1. Explain the current state for this topic in your relationship (e.g. I feel anxious about sharing my concerns with you and end up keeping a lot to myself).

_____

_____

_____

_____

_____

_____

2. What are the observed behaviours that caused you to

give the rating you gave? Avoid statements based on presumed intent (do not discuss what you think your partner thought/felt during the experience that caused them to respond that way)- stick only to the things that happened.

_____

_____

_____

_____

_____

_____

3. Explain what your picture of the ideal state would be for this topic. Give examples of ways you or your partner could get a better score. (e.g. I would like it if you texted me during the day to tell me that you were thinking of me).

_____

_____

_____

_____

_____

_____

_____

_____

_____

_____

Topic:

_____

1. Explain the current state for this topic in your relationship (e.g. I feel anxious about sharing my concerns with you and end up keeping a lot to myself).

_____

_____

_____

_____

_____

_____

_____

2. What are the observed behaviours that caused you to give the rating you gave? Avoid statements based on presumed intent (do not discuss what you think your partner thought/felt during the experience that caused them to respond that way)- stick only to the things that happened.

_____

_____

_____

_____

_____

_____

3. Explain what your picture of the ideal state would be for this topic. Give examples of ways you or your partner could get a better score. (e.g. I would like it if you texted me during the day to tell me that you were thinking of me).

_____

_____

_____

_____

_____

_____

_____

_____

_____

Topic: _____

   1. Explain the current state for this topic in your relationship (e.g. I feel anxious about sharing my concerns with you and end up keeping a lot to myself).

_____

_____

_____

_____

_____

_____

_____

   2. What are the observed behaviours that caused you to give the rating you gave? Avoid statements based on presumed intent (do not discuss what you think your partner thought/felt during the experience that caused them to respond that way)-stick only to the things that happened.

_____

_____

_____

_____

_____

_____

_____

   3. Explain what your picture of the ideal state would be for this topic. Give examples of ways you or your partner could get a better score. (e.g. I would like it if you texted me during the day to tell me that you were thinking of me).

_____

———————————————————————————

———————————————————————————

———————————————————————————

———————————————————————————

———————————————————————————

———————————————————————————

———————————————————————————

———————————————————————————

———————————————————————————

Reflection

After your discussion, go to your own space and reflect on the following points. Ten reflection pages are included, but feel free to print more if you need them.

1) What did you hear from your partner?

2) What new things about yourself or your partner did you learn during today's discussion?

3) What did it seem like your partner cared about the most? What made them the most emotional, animated, or anxious when they were discussing it?

4) Are there any elements about your intent or behaviour that you think your partner doesn't understand (e.g. the points that you may have wanted to interrupt your partner to make during the discussion)?

Create an action plan! Consider "how can I modify my behaviour to be a better partner?"

Write these down as well, and feel free to modify them as much as you need to as your thinking may change as you give it more time. Tomorrow, take time to share these reflections.

Make sure that you have given yourself the day to reflect on what was covered and what you want to say before rushing into the conversation.

After your sharing session, agree on the topics for the next day. The initial sharing session should take place after each partner has had enough time to deeply consider the topics and write out their thoughts, and the reflection sharing session should take place the next day. It is up to you how often you hold these sessions, but do not do more than two topics per session so that you give yourselves the opportunity to truly digest all of the information that will be shared.

For additional copies of this exercise, visit www.findfixforward.com/resources and click on Exercise 14.

Topic: _____

1) What did you hear from your partner?

_____
_____
_____
_____
_____
_____
_____

2) What new things about yourself or your partner did you learn during today's discussion?

_____
_____
_____
_____
_____
_____

3) What did it seem like your partner cared about the most? What made them the most emotional, animated, or anxious when they were discussing it?

_____

_____

_____

_____

_____

4) Are there any elements about your intent or behaviour that you think your partner doesn't understand (e.g. the points that you may have wanted to interrupt your partner to make during the discussion)?

_____

_____

_____

_____

_____

5) Create an action plan! Consider "how can I modify my behaviour to be a better partner?"

_____

_____

_____

_____

_____

_____

Topic: _____
1) What did you hear from your partner?

_____

_____

_____

_____

_____

_____

2) What new things about yourself or your partner did you learn during today's discussion?

_____

_____

_____

_____

_____

3) What did it seem like your partner cared about the most? What made them the most emotional, animated, or anxious when they were discussing it?

_____

_____

_____

_____

_____

4) Are there any elements about your intent or behaviour that you think your partner doesn't understand (e.g. the points that you may have wanted to interrupt your partner to make during the discussion)?

_____

_____

_____

_____

_____

_____

_____

5) Create an action plan! Consider "how can I modify my behaviour to be a better partner?"

_____

_____

_____

_____

_____

_____

_____

Topic: _____

1) What did you hear from your partner?

_____

_____

_____

_____

_____

2) What new things about yourself or your partner did you learn during today's discussion?

_____

_____

_____

_____

_____

3) What did it seem like your partner cared about the most? What made them the most emotional, animated, or

anxious when they were discussing it?

_____

_____

_____

_____

_____

4) Are there any elements about your intent or behaviour that you think your partner doesn't understand (e.g. the points that you may have wanted to interrupt your partner to make during the discussion)?

_____

_____

_____

_____

_____

5) Create an action plan! Consider "how can I modify my behaviour to be a better partner?"

_____

_____

_____

_____

_____

_____

Topic: _____

1) What did you hear from your partner?

_____

_____

_____

_____

_____

_____

2) What new things about yourself or your partner did you learn during today's discussion?

_____

_____

_____

_____

_____

3) What did it seem like your partner cared about the most? What made them the most emotional, animated, or anxious when they were discussing it?

_____

_____

_____

_____

_____

4) Are there any elements about your intent or behaviour that you think your partner doesn't understand (e.g. the points that you may have wanted to interrupt your partner to make during the discussion)?

_____

_____

_____

_____

_____

5) Create an action plan! Consider "how can I modify my

behaviour to be a better partner?"

_____

_____

_____

_____

_____

_____

Topic: _____

1) What did you hear from your partner?

_____

_____

_____

_____

_____

2) What new things about yourself or your partner did you learn during today's discussion?

_____

_____

_____

_____

_____

3) What did it seem like your partner cared about the most? What made them the most emotional, animated, or anxious when they were discussing it?

_____

_____

_____

_____

_____

_____

4) Are there any elements about your intent or behaviour that you think your partner doesn't understand (e.g. the points that you may have wanted to interrupt your partner to make during the discussion)?

_____

_____

_____

_____

_____

5) Create an action plan! Consider "how can I modify my behaviour to be a better partner?"

_____

_____

_____

_____

_____

_____

Topic:

_____

1) What did you hear from your partner?

_____

_____

_____

_____

_____

2) What new things about yourself or your partner did you

learn during today's discussion?

_____

_____

_____

_____

_____

3) What did it seem like your partner cared about the most? What made them the most emotional, animated, or anxious when they were discussing it?

_____

_____

_____

_____

_____

4) Are there any elements about your intent or behaviour that you think your partner doesn't understand (e.g. the points that you may have wanted to interrupt your partner to make during the discussion)?

_____

_____

_____

_____

_____

5) Create an action plan! Consider "how can I modify my behaviour to be a better partner?"

_____

_____

_____

_____

_____

_____

Topic:
_____

1) What did you hear from your partner?

_____

_____

_____

_____

_____

2) What new things about yourself or your partner did you learn during today's discussion?

_____

_____

_____

_____

_____

3) What did it seem like your partner cared about the most? What made them the most emotional, animated, or anxious when they were discussing it?

_____

_____

_____

_____

_____

4) Are there any elements about your intent or behaviour

that you think your partner doesn't understand (e.g. the points that you may have wanted to interrupt your partner to make during the discussion)?

_____

_____

_____

_____

_____

_____

5) Create an action plan! Consider "how can I modify my behaviour to be a better partner?"

_____

_____

_____

_____

_____

_____

_____

Topic: _____

1) What did you hear from your partner?

_____

_____

_____

_____

_____

_____

2) What new things about yourself or your partner did you learn during today's discussion?

_____

_____

_____

_____

_____

_____

3) What did it seem like your partner cared about the most? What made them the most emotional, animated, or anxious when they were discussing it?

_____

_____

_____

_____

_____

4) Are there any elements about your intent or behaviour that you think your partner doesn't understand (e.g. the points that you may have wanted to interrupt your partner to make during the discussion)?

_____

_____

_____

_____

_____

5) Create an action plan! Consider "how can I modify my behaviour to be a better partner?"

_____

_____

_____

_____

_____

_____

Topic: _____

    1) What did you hear from your partner?

_____

_____

_____

_____

_____

    2) What new things about yourself or your partner did you learn during today's discussion?

_____

_____

_____

_____

_____

    3) What did it seem like your partner cared about the most? What made them the most emotional, animated, or anxious when they were discussing it?

_____

_____

_____

_____

_____

    4) Are there any elements about your intent or behaviour that you think your partner doesn't understand (e.g. the points that you may have wanted to interrupt your partner to make during the discussion)?

_____

_____

_____

_____

_____

5) Create an action plan! Consider "how can I modify my behaviour to be a better partner?"

_____

_____

_____

_____

_____

_____

Topic:_____

1) What did you hear from your partner?

_____

_____

_____

_____

_____

2) What new things about yourself or your partner did you learn during today's discussion?

_____

_____

_____

_____

_____

3) What did it seem like your partner cared about the most? What made them the most emotional, animated, or anxious when they were discussing it?

_____

_____

_____

_____

_____

_____

4) Are there any elements about your intent or behaviour that you think your partner doesn't understand (e.g. the points that you may have wanted to interrupt your partner to make during the discussion)?

_____

_____

_____

_____

_____

_____

5) Create an action plan! Consider "how can I modify my behaviour to be a better partner?"

_____

_____

_____

_____

_____

_____

Wrap Up!

Congratulations on putting in all of that hard work and allowing yourself to be so open and vulnerable! If you completed all of the exercises in this book, you should have an amazing foundation for moving forward on the path towards fulfilment. Your final exercise will be to create an all-inclusive action plan for the items you agreed throughout the various exercises that you would do as individuals and as a couple. Let's take a moment to zoom out and reflect on what we learned.

For additional copies of this exercise, visit www.findfixforward.com/resources and click on Exercise 15.

Your Key Takeaways

What did you learn during the exercises? What were your biggest "a-ha" moments that you didn't know about before? These could be lessons about yourself, your partner, or you as a couple.

_____

_____

_____

_____

_____

_____

_____

_____

_____

_____

_____

_____

_____

_____

_____

_____

Unresolved Issues

Is there anything that you think was left unsaid or unresolved?
Did you not push as hard as you wanted to get the answers you
wanted, or did you not share all you had to say? If there is
anything you still haven't gotten to the bottom of, write it here.

_____

_____

_____

_____

_____

_____

_____

_____

_____

_____

_____

_____

_____

_____

_____

_____

_____

_____

_____

_____

_____

_____

_____

_____

_____

_____

_____

_____

_____

_____

Action Plan

Now, what are you going to do about it? Go back to the plans you made throughout the book and put them all in one place. Use the lines below, write it in a notebook, or get a tattoo with it all listed — whatever works best for you. Make sure that the actions you have suggested are things you can follow through on and are measurable. After sharing your action plans, check back regularly to keep each other accountable.

_____

Team Share

Throughout these exercises, you have developed some great strategies for communicating and sharing with your partner. Now it's time to use them! Share your takeaways, which will help your partner feel heard and understood. Share any unresolved issues, which will allow for opportunities to clear up any issues that are lingering. Finally, share your action plan. Pledge to your partner what you intend to do in order to continue your improved level of communication, clarity, and openness. These plans should be referenced and checked often, as humans tend to revert back into old habits and ways of behaving. When you are finished, enjoy a well-deserved celebration together!

Conclusion

It is my most sincere hope that this book helped you to get clarity. Whether you are looking towards a bright future together as a new couple or you are a couple working through issues built up over time, I hope that the exercises in this book have helped you to get to know and understand yourself more deeply. The most important relationship in your life is the one you have with yourself, so being honest about who you are and what you want, at least with yourself, is the first step to happiness and true fulfilment. Thank you for your bravery, courage, and openness throughout this process, and I wish you the very best on your journey, wherever it may take you.

CPSIA information can be obtained
at www.ICGtesting.com
Printed in the USA
BVHW082023011221
622869BV00008B/226